MOVING BORDERS

MOVING BORDERS

The life story of Josephine Tramer

Annie Louisa Harrison

BREWIN BOOKS

First published by
Brewin Books Ltd, 56 Alcester Road,
Studley, Warwickshire B80 7LG in 2016
www.brewinbooks.com

ISBN: 978-1-85858-558-1

A Cataloguing in Publication Record
for this title is available from the British Library.

Typeset in Haarlemmer MT Std
Printed in Great Britain by
Bell & Bain Ltd.

Contents

Acknowledgements

My thanks to all the people who have helped me:

My friend, Angela Roberts who tirelessly, read and translated German documents.

Dr. Michaela Laichman MAS –Vienna State Archive.

DSA Irma Wulz BA, Vienna Jewish Records Office whom I am sure did more than routine work to help me.

Magistrat der Stadt, Vienna.

The Jewish Community of Vienna Museum, where I was left with my thoughts and aided in my research.

The Budapest Great Synagogue Staff who not only showed me around the Jewish quarter but helped me to understand the work between Gentiles and Jews in an attempt to save lives.

Roger Armstrong, Jo's solicitor from Keighley West Yorkshire, who helped me to obtain Jo's Army records. I know that he did far more work for Jo than was professionally expected.

The Vienna Schonbrunn Palace guide who spent time looking at and dating photographs.

The Reichstag Museum in Berlin who helped me to understand a little of the issues involved in a nation trying to make sense of its history.

The British Army Personnel Centre Glasgow.

Jean Garbutt, Jo's long term friend and supporter, who provided stories, photographs and cartoons that helped me to understand 'the girl behind this woman'.

Michael Chirzan who drove me to and around Bielsko-Biala. His persistence helped me to find the Aleksandrowice cemetery.

Henryk Drzewiecki, the caretaker of the cemetery, who was the first person to locate evidence of Moses' death.

The International Jewish Cemetery Project.

Stanley Diamond, Executive Director, Jewish Records Indexing Poland, who put me in touch with Jacek Prosyck. Jacek's research into the history of people buried in the Aleksandrowice cemetery provided valuable information about Moses Tramer and his family.

Guides at the Castle Wawel in Krakow.

This book is dedicated to Josephine Tramer who became Josephine Telford. She left me the tools to write this story but was not here to read or correct it.

Foreword

This is the story of Josephine Tramer who died on 5th March 2010. She was one hundred years old. She was part of my life for over twenty years. When she died she left me enough information to start filling in many of the gaps in her story. Her country was Austria. We who live on an island, with some history of border issues, have no idea of the consequences of relentless changing of borders and political domination.

I do not pretend that Jo's story is unique. It has taken victims over half a century to start telling their stories. Jo told many stories but decided to leave only clues that led me to what I suspected already. She was a strong woman who was not going to be defeated by Hitler or anyone else.

My research has been about the life of one woman and, of course, I have learned many things about the persecution of a race. This is not an academic tome. Having said that, I have done my best to convey faithfully the information that has been given to me. On the way I have shed many tears and thanked God for His goodness. As Jo said many times, "Thank the Good Lord that I am here".

Chapter 1

Our heroine

The telephone rang on 2nd February 1998. "It is me, Jo," she said. "I have been mugged." I expressed my shock and asked if she was all right. She said, "I went to town to pay bills. A young woman asked if I had change for a pound. I took out my purse and she grabbed it. I held on to the purse with one hand. With the other I hit her in the face, and then I hit her again. A car stopped and a man got out and held onto the woman. Another man stopped. He called the police on his mobile phone."

Jo was eighty eight years old, less than five feet tall and of slight build. The offending young woman was arrested and initially pleaded 'not guilty'. When Jo said she would give evidence the woman changed her plea to guilty. She went to prison.

The story illustrates the essence of this woman. She had come through too much to be defeated by someone who was prepared to take her money in the street. I had long been telling her that it was not safe to be wandering around paying bills with cash. She said that, for her, going out to pay bills gave some purpose to her life. She enjoyed using the bus, meeting people and buying herself some lunch.

Jo was in her late seventies when I first met her. I attended a congregational chapel in an English village. She appeared at chapel one Sunday. She had lived in the village for some years. People knew her. She was part of village life and in her time had helped with delivering meals on wheels and the 'Old People's Welfare Service'. She came to the chapel having been invited by one of the members called Jack. He delivered fruit and vegetables and frequently invited people to 'come and join us'. She

The tin box.

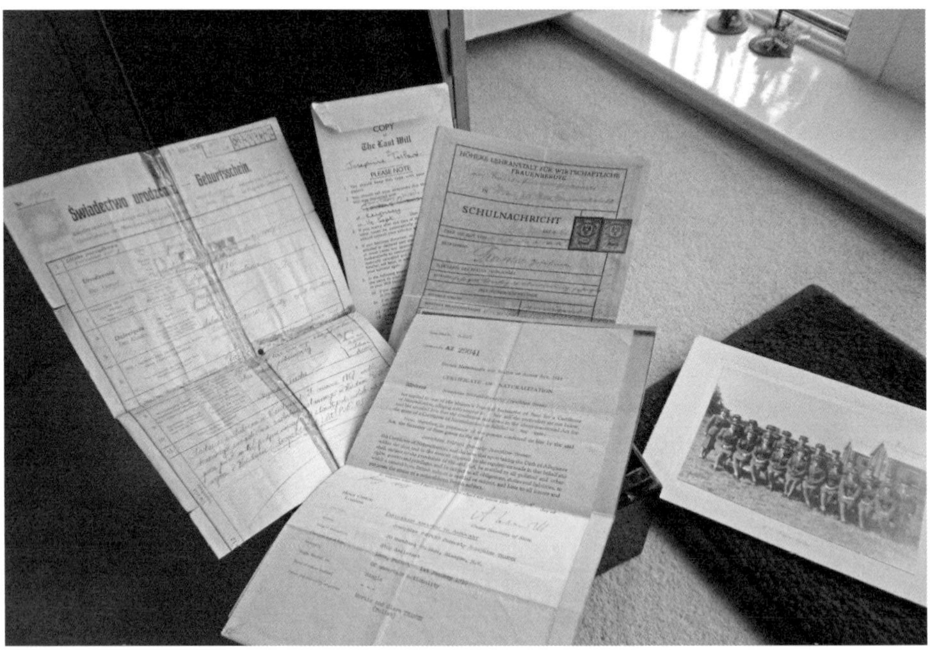

The contents of the tin box.

fitted in to chapel life. She became a member and attended regularly, even after leaving the village and later when she needed support in looking after herself. One day she said, "You know this was not my religion". I waited for the next line but it never came.

Jo talked about her history but I knew that many things were left unsaid. She talked about an ex colleague giving her a tin box in which to store her documents. She did not show the box to me. She said she was from Vienna and one day would like to take me there.

Jo died on 5th March 2010. She was one hundred years old. She left a detailed will asking for her funeral service to be conducted in the congregational chapel. I had the great honour of arranging and conducting that funeral service. In my preparation for the service I was handed the tin box and later told that it was mine to keep. I could have called this account 'a journey from a tin box'. There was enough information contained in the box for me to research her history. I suspect that she did not know some aspects of her history. She did take me to Vienna but not until after her death.

Chapter 2

The Austro-Hungarian Empire

On 26th June 1907, at a Jewish ceremony in Vienna, Klara Kraus, the daughter of Solomon and Fanni Kraus, married Moses Tramer, the son of Mark and Perl Tramer. Klara was twenty four years old and her new husband was ten years her senior. I have found differing ways of spelling Moses' name. 'Moses' is the spelling on his marriage certificate and in the absence of any direction to the contrary, I will use this throughout.

Birth records confirm that Klara came from Vienna. Her husband came from a family that, for a number of generations, had lived in Bielitz. This Polish town was in Upper Silesia. Jo was born in Lemberg. This was also a Polish town. The reader might experience some confusion with my use of the word 'was'. The three locations mentioned, at the time of Jo's birth, were all part of the Austro-Hungarian Empire. A railway line joins the three places. Moses was a businessman or salesman. Bielitz was a thriving industrial town. It is, therefore, easy to understand how, in the course of his business, he would travel to Vienna. There may also have been close ties between his and Klara's families. Lemberg, renamed Lwow after World War I, was a relatively short distance from Bielitz. The family moved to Bielitz when Jo was three years old.

In 1918 Poland, which had a long history of being occupied and controlled by foreign powers, was reconstituted as an independent state. In order to work in Poland people had to take Polish Nationality. Klara and Moses did this. There are records of the couple living in Bielitz. The records say that the family moved to Vienna in 1924. It is not clear as to how the family's time was divided between Bielitz and Vienna. Jo's school reports show that from the age of fifteen she was being educated in Vienna. Other records show Klara being in Bielitz after this date. Moses ended his life in Bielitz. It appears that Klara was in Vienna at that time. My interpretation of the situation is that the family's 'heart' was in Vienna but Moses had to maintain a base in Bielitz to protect his occupation. Jo, in later years, used to say, "Because of my father's work I was born in Poland". Bielitz and Bielsko are the same place. I will return to this point later. Early British documents show Jo's nationality as being 'uncertain'.

Lwow, now Lvov, is part of the Ukraine. Jo always said she was Austrian and from Vienna. To clarify, her place of birth was part of the Austro-Hungarian Empire and that became part of the new Polish State and is now in the Ukraine.

The guides at the Castel Wawel in Krakow were very helpful in helping me to understand Polish history. The consensus of opinion appears to be that the Austrian authorities were fairly liberal occupiers. Polish culture was allowed to flourish and even the activities of the independence movement were tolerated.

Chapter 3

Jewish history in Austria and Poland

I was born eight years after the end of World War II. Rationing of some products had not quite come to an end. The war was a major topic of conversation. Most houses had photographs of servicemen on their walls. I knew that many of the men depicted had died serving their country. As a small child I was taken to visit relatives in Coventry which had suffered as a result of heavy bombing by German planes. We then moved to Coventry and there were many bombsites which were great places to play. Coventry Cathedral stands as a great monument to renewal after intended destruction. For us, war was about dropping bombs and protecting our land from the Germans. We were taught something about concentration camps and the persecution of the Jews. We knew that people were murdered in gas chambers. Nothing prepared me for the magnitude of death, suffering and hate that I learned about whilst preparing this history. The first thing to hit me was the vast numbers of people killed. Believe me when I say that, in no way, am I prepared to let Adolf Hitler off the hook. Nevertheless, the history of racism and persecution long predates him. He also had many, many, culpable people who helped.

The first written record of a Jewish person in Vienna is in 1190. In 1421 Jews were expelled from Vienna. One hundred and eighty years later Jewish people were allowed to reform communities. They were needed as financiers. I can hardly believe the distorted reasoning behind this. The 'authority' is to be found in the Old Testament. I quote from the King James translation of the Bible. Deuteronomy chapter 23 verses 19 and 20 state 'Thou shalt not lend upon usury to thy brother' and 'Unto a stranger thou mayest lend upon usury'. For 'usury' read 'monetary interest'. Therefore, the authorities decided it was better to export the role of financier onto another race. Hence, the Jews got the job. I wonder if the stereotype of the Jewish banker was in fact created rather than observed by Gentiles. Somewhere along the line the concept of the dishonest moneylender was developed. I fail to grasp how, what I understand, to be an instruction to lend money to ones' relatives without charging interest was somehow changed. The change amounted to fellow Gentiles being ones' brothers and the Jews being strangers even if they were ones' neighbours. Add distrust of bankers to misuse of both Old and New Testament teaching and one has elements of Nazi doctrine.

Before leaving the subject of money, it should be pointed out that the most important Baroque church in Vienna was co-financed by German Jews. The privilege of residence in Vienna cost the Jews 150,000 guilders. A substantial Jewish loan made possible the building of the Schonbrunn Palace in around 1750.

In 1624 the Jews had to leave again and went to a ghetto in Unterer Werd. In 1670 Leopold I decided to expel the Jews again. In 1782 there was an Edict of Tolerance. A third community was established in 1852 and before 1900 this was the third largest Jewish community in Europe. In 1867, for the first time, every person in the monarchy was deemed to be Equal Before the Law. Vienna became a city of immigrants. In 1880 sixty percent of the population had not been born there.

Some 300,000 Jews were brought into the Austrian Imperial Army in World War I. Of these 25,000 were officers. Moses Tramer completed military service and was decorated with three medals. Military service accompanied a false hope of equal treatment. The collapse of the multi-ethnic Habsburg Empire in 1918, whilst creating a nation state, did not provide for the protection of minorities. This proved detrimental for the Jews. The Jewish community in Vienna was brutally destroyed in 1938.

A statement I found in the Jewish Museum in Vienna announced what needed to be said. In 1991 Franz Vranitzky was the first Austrian Federal Chancellor to speak of the shared responsibility of Austrians during the

Nazi era. For years Austria had claimed to be the first victim of Nazi-ism. In 1956, 1962 and 1976 'small assistance payments' were paid to Austrian Jewish people in need all over the world. Politicians never spoke of compensation. In 1998 the Art Restitution Act created an effective means of tracing mobile, looted property instead of just real estate and liquidated companies.

Bielsko, once part of the Czech State and Austro-Hungarian Empire, was a small town in southern Poland on the river Biala. It was once known as the town of one hundred industries. Until 1951 the towns of Bielsko and Biala, separated by the river, belonged to separate provinces. They are now one town, Bielsko-Biala. The town has many similarities to British industrial towns, there is a large civic hall and church and it is busy with shops catering for the needs of the population. There is evidence of industrial activity including wool and cloth production.

Jews settled in Bielsko in the second half of the seventeenth century. The first mention of them is in 1653. In 1819 Kaiser France Joseph I granted permission for a second market day to be held on Wednesdays. This was important as the only other market day had been Saturday, the Jewish Sabbath. The constitution of 1849 gave equal rights to all citizens of Austria. By the second half of the nineteenth century the area enjoyed a significant degree of autonomy as part of Cieszyn, Silesia and Galacia. Jo said she was born and spent much of her childhood in Silesia. In later life she was on holiday in Austria when someone recognized her accent as being Silesian. It was an irritation to her that, despite living in Britain for over sixty years, she had not managed to lose her accent.

After World War I in 1918, and the dissolution of the Austro-Hungarian Empire, the Polish State was reconstituted. I can imagine, after years of occupation, this must have been a time for celebration in Poland. Sadly, history teaches us that there are negative consequences to what, on the face of it, are positive changes. Not all citizens were pleased with the new Polish State. To work in Poland one had to become a Polish citizen. Klara and Moses were no exception. Jo was eight years old. I have not found any documents to say that her nationality was changed. In fact, when she took British nationality, her nationality of origin was given as 'unspecific'.

Ethnic Germans in Poland formed anti-Polish and anti-Jewish organizations. The German Ministry of Foreign Affairs sponsored their activities. Britain's engagement in World War II followed the annexing of Poland by Nazi Germany. 'Annexing' is quite a spine chilling word. It seeks to neutralize the obliteration of another country and race. Of course, the racism against the Jews, long predated Adolf Hitler.

Prior to the invasion of the German Army on 3rd September 1939 most Jews fled the town of Bielsko but many returned when the advancing German Army prevented them leaving. The Judenrat was created at the end of 1939 and a ghetto established in the summer of 1941. This was 'liquidated' in June 1942 and the remaining four hundred Jews deported to Auschwitz. 'Liquidated', how can this be a word for the destruction of a people?

In researching this history I have wandered about, notebook in hand, recording what I felt to be relevant. In Auschwitz I took no notes. The whole process seemed too important for selective note taking. I took no photographs inside the buildings. I have no idea if photographs were allowed. The emotion I felt was 'anger'. The tears came later. How could this happen? Who let it happen?

I was driven to Auschwitz by car. We passed little villages and green fields. I learned that the Nazis cleared the surrounding areas. To be clear, people were moved out of the area so that this place could be allowed to function 'secretly'. Did no-one notice that this was strange? The commandant lived in a large house next to the perimeter wall. His wife lived with him. The upstairs windows of the house overlooked the wall. Those windows afforded a view of his eventual execution.

Initially, Auschwitz was reserved for the thinkers and academics of society. Apparently the real aim of the Nazis was to clear Poland of Poles.

Chapter 4

Josephine

Jo's parents were married on 26th June 1907. Their union was conducted in a Jewish ceremony in Vienna. Their parents and other family members were present. Her father, Moses, came from Bielsko. On some documents his first name is given as Moritz. His cemetery record gives his name as Mojzess. Travelling in Poland I met men who gave their names in three different ways. The names varied in a similar way to those used by Moses. When I asked what they would like me to call them they chose the one that they thought would be correct for my culture. This did not appear to be a problem and reflected changes in language and culture over time.

There are records showing that Moses came from a well-established family in Bielsko. As the wedding was in Vienna and Jo always said she was from Vienna I can only assume that her mother Klara's family was established there.

Jo said that 'because of her father's work' she was born in Poland. Until researching his history I had assumed that he moved to Poland to find work. This does not appear to be the case. His family is from Bielsko. Jo was born in Lemberg. This is a relatively short distance from Bielsko. In fact Jo and her parents moved to Bielsko when Jo was three years old. Jo said that her father was a businessman. Records say he was a salesman. Bielsko was a place of industry, the railway line connected Vienna, Bielsko and Lemberg. It may be that the families were connected in some way. Alternatively, Moses may have met Klara when he travelled to Vienna on business. I am advised that the Jewish communities in Vienna and Bielsko were more

Photograph of Josephine aged 3 years old taken at Lwow.

relaxed in their faith than some orthodox communities. The fact that Moses was some ten years older than Klara suggests some family involvement in the marriage arrangements.

Jo did not talk about her father or repeat anything he might have said. She frequently talked about her mother and their home. The house they lived in had a stove. I once took a photograph of a stove in Finland and took it to show Jo. She confirmed that this was the correct item. I am now reliably informed that many Polish homes still have a stove. This is a sort of central heating system. The fire is lit in an oven, at a central position, on the lowest floor. From the chimney other rooms have metal doors that can be opened when needed. The efficiency of the system is in being able to direct and control the heat as necessary. If this makes no sense a visit to the Castle Wawel in Krakow will make matters clear.

The impression I have is of a family home where there were standards. Jo said her mother would not let her have second helpings at meal times. She would say, "You have had enough". This instilled into Jo a lifetime habit of not being greedy as far as food was concerned.

Official written records provided by Jo say that the family moved back to Vienna in 1924. Other records show that Moses and, sometimes, Klara were in Bielitz. The only explanation I can offer is that Moses, because of his work, needed to have a base in Bielitz. The main family home was in Vienna.

I have copies of Jo's school/college reports for 1925 and 1926. By this time she was being educated in Vienna at The Women's Higher Education Facility. She attended a course for women intending a career in business. She was studying to become a shorthand typist. Her academic record was good. She told me that her mother sent her on a course to learn to type. This skill, along with her language skills, proved invaluable. She wisely took her certificates with her when she left Austria. The original certificates were in the tin box.

The Vienna Jewish Records Office was able to locate documents relating to Jo's successful application for an Austrian Pension. Amongst the documents was Jo's sworn affidavit in support of her application. She states that between September 1927 and June 1938 she worked, as a shorthand typist, for the firm of Kohlen-und Oelfirma Ad. Schramek, in Vienna.

I have photographs of people skiing. I am sure that one of them is of Jo, another is of a man and a woman on skis. On the back of the photograph is written, Wislunaeltew 1937.

On the back of a photograph of two girls is the year 1935. The girls are sitting on rocks, one of them could be Jo.

Jo skiing.

Wislunaeltew 1937.

Climbing during 1935.

On her pension application Jo states that she was persecuted, between the 5th March 1933 and the 8th May 1945, on political grounds and because of her place of birth. The dates are part of the application form rather than actual dates of persecution. She came to England on the 17th May 1939.

Jo frequently talked about her political activity. She talked about lying behind barbed wire fences and throwing hand grenades. There was nothing tragic in the way she told these stories, the sense was one of adventure. Her stories were about fighting the Germans because they were the enemy. She never spoke, to me, about being persecuted because of her religion or place of birth. I find a deep sadness in this. It was not safe enough to tell the whole story even to someone who had known intimate details about her. I have been informed that she did confide in one or two people who in some way shared her history. I cannot give an account of this because the information has no detail and is, by now, third hand.

By 1939 Jo had, at least, two skirmishes with the authorities. There is now no doubt that 'the authorities' were not just German occupiers. Her mother felt that it was unsafe for Jo to remain in Austria and an application was made for her to become an au pair in England. This was a way of young people obtaining free board and lodging in return for domestic duties. If they had been employees they would have needed work permits. In preparation for this position her mother sent her on a course to learn how to iron men's dress shirts. Well, I know nothing about 1940s dress shirts but have tried to iron the more modern variety, what a nightmare task! Anyway, the whole course was a waste of time and effort. In Jo's words her new 'employer', as she saw him, came home 'mucked up'. Whatever his employment he was not required to wear a dress shirt. One can imagine Jo's mother thinking that her daughter was to work in a grand house with very high standards. I have seen the exterior of the house. It is large and positioned in the countryside. There is no doubt that the owners were relatively affluent.

Many young people had harsh words to say about the people who benefited from their au pair work. Jo had no such complaints. The family lived in Bingley, West Yorkshire. This is an old market town in the Aire Valley. Their home was positioned about a mile above the town in surrounding countryside. Jo's tasks included bringing coal into the house and looking after a little boy. I remember that 'little boy' visiting her when she was living in warden-controlled accommodation. She said that she shed tears when she saw him. I do not recall her talking about shedding tears over anything else. Whenever we passed the road where the family had lived she said, "That is the first place I lived in Yorkshire". She loved Yorkshire because, she said, it reminded her of Austria. As far as I know Jo did not visit the family after she finished working for them.

There is a wonderful photograph of Jo dressed for housework. She is wearing a wrap-around pinafore and headscarf. This was the attire of many women to prevent damaging their other clothes when performing household tasks. Behind Jo there is a pram and a line of washing.

I hardly ever saw Jo when she did not mention Austria. She had a lifetime interest in skiing. She skied well into her fifties and afterwards enjoyed watching the sport on television. She frequently mentioned Vienna but rarely spoke about a specific location for skiing. She travelled back to Vienna many times, the focus of these visits was to speak with her lawyer.

Jo in her au pair uniform.

The lawyer was instrumental in her obtaining an Austrian pension. Yorkshire had a long tradition of manufacturing high quality woollen goods. She always took a suit length of cloth as a gift for her lawyer. These visits ceased as she became older. She discovered that the Austrian authorities were satisfied if a British lawyer or the British Police certified annually that she was still alive.

In May 1940 Jo was arrested from her home in Bingley. Along with many other people from Austria, and territories thought to be a risk, she was interned on the Isle of Man. I expressed horror when she told me about this. She said, "It was better than being an au pair in Bingley". This was not a reflection on the family she lived with but an acknowledgement of the way she was treated on the Isle of Man. An area of the island was cordoned off. Guesthouses and hotels were used to accommodate the detainees. Jo must have felt fear when she was arrested. She must have had some awareness of the plight of political prisoners in her homeland. She was released in March 1941 and returned to her former home in Bingley.

On 7th August 1941 Jo enlisted in the Auxiliary Territorial Service of the British Army. She was very proud to wear the British uniform. One did not have to be with her for long before being told about her army service. Her army record shows that her clerical skills were used. On a record card her 'sports played' are given as swimming, skiing and climbing. There may have been a little creative detail here. She told me that her mother made her learn to

Jo from her Austrian Alpine pass 1959.

swim but she really hated the activity. The other two activities were regularly enjoyed. In addition to English her spoken languages are given as German, French, Italian and Dutch. She was qualified to drive a motorcycle and a lorry.

It is interesting to note that a comment on the top of her Service and Casualty form are the words 'only to be employed as cook or orderly'. A note dated 25th July 1942 says she passed the trade test as clerk. The record says she changed her name to Telford on 19th May 1944.

One of Jo's army friends, Donald Fraser Capt. RE, drew cartoons of her. One is dated 7-2-44. It shows Jo arriving for duty, her suitcase says 'Wien' (Vienna) on it and in German she says 'I thought roses grew in England'. Others, undated, show her at her pay office desk. On one she is running away from a cow. The cartoons suggest a happy relationship with the artist. She kept the pictures for many years before giving them to her friend Jean for safekeeping.

On reviewing the documents it occurs to me that Jo did not give too much detail about her first period of Army service. Along with two other war medals she was awarded the France and Germany Star. This medal was awarded for operational service in France, Belgium, Luxemburg, the Netherlands and Germany from June 1944 to May 1945.

The army extended her service by two years. An entry in her Army record dated 25th January 1946 says she was posted to No. 2 War Office ATS Records Telegram DVI. In February 1946 she was sent to Belgium and then to Germany. On 25th March 1946 she was posted to No. 1 Control Comm. for Germany. She spoke a little about this work. She looked after an appointment system for German military personnel. She said that, the higher the rank of the officer, the longer she kept them waiting. She never repeated or talked about what she may have heard or seen at work, during this time.

One day Jo was waiting on a railway platform in Germany. She was wearing her army uniform. She heard someone say 'English pigs'. She turned and in German, said, "We British understand German very well". I'm not sure that we are best known for our language skills but appreciate the vote of confidence! She must have been a great asset to the army at that time.

When Jo enlisted in 1941 she gave her religion as Jewish. She was posted to various units including Harrogate and York. With her extended period of service her discharge date is given as 25th April 1948.

'I thought roses grew in England'.

'Sick Pay'.

Too much paperwork.

Left: A tidy desk. Right: A quick escape.

Jo, front row, left, and her medals.

Army group planning in Europe.

Light hearted relief for the girls.

Army photograph with Jo seated, front row, on the far right.

At some point, after the end of the war, Jo returned to Vienna to look for her mother. Amongst Jo's documents is a Vienna pass. It states that she is a member of the Vienna Garrison, gives her service record number, and states that she is a corporal. Sadly the document is not dated. I have photographs showing service men and women, including Jo. They are informally but uniformly dressed. They are standing in front of a building with a German business sign. This could have been taken in Austria. It is likely that Jo went to look for her mother when she was off duty whilst serving in Europe. We know that she was, at some point, staying with the Vienna Garrison.

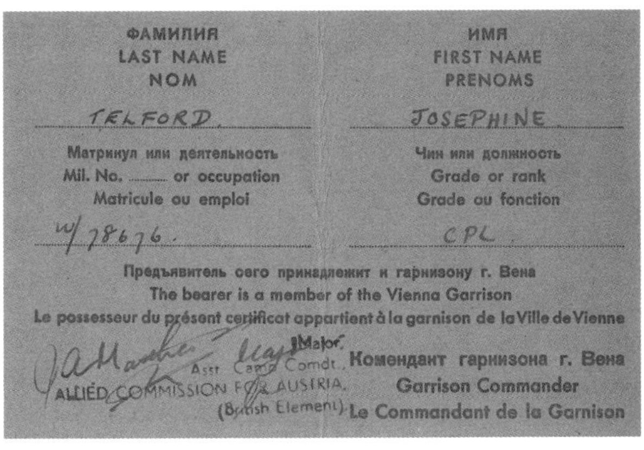

ФАМИЛИЯ
LAST NAME
NOM

TELFORD

ИМЯ
FIRST NAME
PRENOMS

JOSEPHINE

Матрикул или деятельность
Mil. No. .... or occupation
Matricule ou emploi

W/78676.

Чин или должность
Grade or rank
Grade ou fonction

CPL.

Предъявитель сего принадлежит к гарнизону г. Вена
The bearer is a member of the Vienna Garrison
Le possesseur du présent certificat appartient à la garnison de la Ville de Vienne

Major.
Asst. Camp Comdt.,
ALLIED COMMISSION FOR AUSTRIA.
(British Element).

Комендант гарнизона г. Вена
Garrison Commander
Le Commandant de la Garnison

Vienna Garrison Pass.

Chapter 5

Klara

Klara was born on 9th September 1883. Jo often talked about her mother. She kept her mother's photograph on her dressing table. She was an elegant woman. She made plans to keep her daughter safe.

At the end of the war Jo went to look for her mother. The impression given to me was that her mother had lived in an apartment in Vienna. It is possible that her father Moses had already died, in Poland, before Jo left Vienna for Britain. The war would have made communication almost impossible. Jo went to where her mother had lived. A neighbour said she had gone and had left a box of belongings for Jo. One wonders whether or not this neighbour was Jewish. The box contained various items including paintings and a ring. At that time Jo's only address belonged to the army. She had no way of keeping paintings so she sold them. She kept the ring and that is now in safe keeping with Jo's long-term friend.

As far as I am aware Jo did not know exactly what happened to her mother. By implication she knew that she had been taken to a concentration camp. Speculation was unspoken. I knew what she suspected but could not say. This all fitted with giving no clues as to her origins for fear of reprisals. I am sure that she did not fear her friends but talk can result in reprisals from one's enemies. There is no evidence that she had any enemies at that time. She was all too aware that it is possible to be betrayed by neighbours and others previously thought of as friends.

On 26th January 1942 Klara was 'deported' from Vienna to the Riga camp in Latvia. She 'did not survive'.

Jo's mother Klara.

In 1935 43,600 Jews lived in Riga. On 1st July 1941 German troops invaded. After many atrocities a ghetto with a surrounding wall was constructed. Late in 1941 an estimated 27,000 Jews were shot in the Rumbola woods. By the end of 1941 deported Jews were thrown into the ghetto or had to do hard labour. Conditions in the ghetto were so poor that the weaker people did not survive. People were marched to the ghetto. Those too weak to walk were offered lifts on trucks. These became known as 'gas trucks'. Out of one thousand people deported from Vienna only 300 reached the ghetto on foot.

As I research this story I am not simply overwhelmed by the number of people and places where these crimes were committed. I am devastated at the number of people who must have known about these atrocities. How can thousands of people be marched through a country, dying as they go, and people just let it happen? No doubt somebody will attempt an explanation. Whatever the explanation is, it cannot be good enough. It must be said that many people took huge risks to protect Jews. Not every German supported Nazi ideals. I recently learned about numbers of Jews being hidden in the crypt of the Church of the Holy Spirit in Heidelberg. Anti-Semitic ideology, even now, is no stranger to Britain.

Jo could not honour her mother with a funeral. She was spoken of at Jo's funeral and her photograph displayed for all to see.

Chapter 6

Moses

Research into Moses' history has taken some time and I have been assisted by a number of people. From conversations with Jo I had assumed that he was Austrian and from Vienna. At the time of his birth he was Austrian as Southern Poland was part of the Austro-Hungarian Empire. He took Polish nationality, when Poland became a republic, in order to remain working in Silesia.

The Jewish Records Office in Vienna promptly provided records relating to Klara and located the certificate of her marriage to Moses. They could not find similar records for Moses. It took some time before I realized that I was searching in the wrong place and started to search in Poland. Information provided by the Magistrat der Stadt in Vienna proved invaluable.

Moses was born on the 18th August 1873 in Galacia, Poland. Between 16th October 1914 and 18th May 1915 he is shown as living with Klara and Jo in a hotel.

There is a photograph of Moses wearing three medals. The medals were dated, for me, by my guide at the Schonbrunn Palace in Vienna. Two medals showed the image of the Emperor Franz Joseph and must have been awarded between 1848 and 1916. The other was a Hungarian medal.

Between 19th July 1924 and 7th January 1925 he is shown as living at an address in Bielitz. Bielitz became Bielsko. Later the towns of Bielsko and Biala joined and became Bielsko-Biala.

Between 7th January 1925 and 13th August 1929 he is shown as 'reporting' with Klara and Jo and an address is given. This period overlaps the time when Jo was at college in Vienna and other records say 'the family' moved to Vienna. The document suggests, but does not say, that this reporting was in Bielitz.

Between 14th August 1929 and 8th September 1930 he is shown as reporting with Klara. A different address is shown. Again the document leads me to believe that this was in Bielitz.

Between 17th March 1938 and 28th March 1938 Moses was in a hospital in the Jewish Community. No indication is given as to his illness. He had another period in hospital from 7th April 1938 to 22nd May 1938. The entry says he 'signed out' of the hospital. I am advised that this is a term used in Poland when someone is discharged or discharges himself from hospital. Information discovered later makes me quite sure that these hospital stays were in Bielitz.

Jo's father Moses.

I went to Poland in order to find the town where Moses had lived. It is now called Bielsko-Biala. The information I gained could not have been done without my driver who spoke perfect English and was interested in my quest. I showed him the addresses where Moses had lived. He said he would do his best but the street names would no longer be the same as they were German names. We went to the town hall to ask if anyone had a map or record of the name changes. It transpired that someone would know but was not available on that day. I was told to send an email in Polish giving my authority for asking the questions. This task, performed to the letter, was unsuccessful.

We walked around the town and I was interested to see what sort of town it was. It was a busy, working town with an impressive town hall. The town had many things in common with Bradford in West Yorkshire. We asked people if there was a synagogue. One man gave us an address. We went there but I was not sure if we had the right place. We asked if there was a Jewish Quarter and were told 'no'. Michael, my driver, was upset on my behalf. He thought my time had been wasted. I assured him that it had not. He then had 'a brain wave'. We saw a woman having a smoke outside of a travel agents' office. He went to speak with her and came back with information. There was a Jewish cemetery just outside of the town. As we approached the cemetery I said, "The Star of David". It was a surprise to see such a prominent symbol in a region that appeared to deny all knowledge of the Jews. The Aleksandrowice Cemetery looked well cared for and was behind iron railings. Hynryk, the caretaker, let us in.

Michael my driver and helper in Poland.

Michael told Hynryk what we were trying to do and Hynryk returned with the cemetery ledger. There he was. Mojzess (Moses) Tramer aged 66 was buried in 1939. Tears flowed on that occasion. Hynryk told us that he could not identify the exact burial plot as there was no grave number. He put us in touch with someone who might be able to give further information. Once again this was unsuccessful. However not only

Aleksandrowice Cemetery signs.

had I found Moses, it was possible that he had not suffered in a concentration camp or some other cruel death.

Whilst this was an amazing result I was to find other shocking information. German troops destroyed and desecrated Jewish graves. Eventually many remains were moved to Aleksandrowice. My research has shown that Jewish organizations kept careful records and research is an ongoing task.

Stanley Diamond, Executive Director of the Jewish Records Indexing Poland, provided crucial information. He told me about the work of Jacek Proszyk who is an expert on the Jewish Community in Bielsko. Jacek's work provided a record of the Tramer family's deaths going back to 1896. Moses and his father are clearly listed. I know that the name Mark/Markus is correct for his father because of the information on Moses and Klara's marriage certificate.

The records clearly indicate that Moses and his family were originally from the Bielsko area and not from Vienna as previously thought. Jo had clearly not wanted to be Polish and never gave any indication of her father originating from Poland. She said, "Because of my father's work I was born in Poland". As far as I know she never revisited Poland.

Chapter 7

Post war civilian life

After her extended period of army service Jo went to live with her cousin in Glasgow. I regret not asking more questions about her cousin. On official forms she is recorded as Mrs. J. Mayer. The most recent address I have is in the Pollockshields area of Glasgow. I do not know if she was a first cousin or which side of Jo's family she came from. Her first and maiden names are not recorded. Jo talked about working with her in a shop selling gloves and handbags. I assumed that her cousin owned the shop. The merchandise was said to be of good quality. Jo loved leather gloves and handbags and often commented on the poor state of my gloves. She was irritated when I refused to let her buy me new ones. She did not appear to grasp the concept of possessions being old friends.

During the time I knew her Jo used to visit her cousin in Glasgow, years before, they were able to go skiing together. Jo enjoyed buying Scottish gifts. I remember these visits coming to an end when her cousin died. From that time she had no living relatives. As I write this I wonder if there is someone out there who is a relative?

Whilst living in Scotland, on 18th July 1947, Jo applied for British Status under the 1914 British Nationality and Status of Aliens Act. On the application form she gives her occupation as shop assistant. She swore her 'faithful and true allegiance to His Majesty King George the Sixth, His Heirs and Successors' on 28th July 1947 in the County of Argyll. Jo expressed her pride in being British. There were never any regrets in taking this step. I have read about some Jewish immigrants becoming 'more British than British'. This was not so in Jo's case. She loved Britain but was

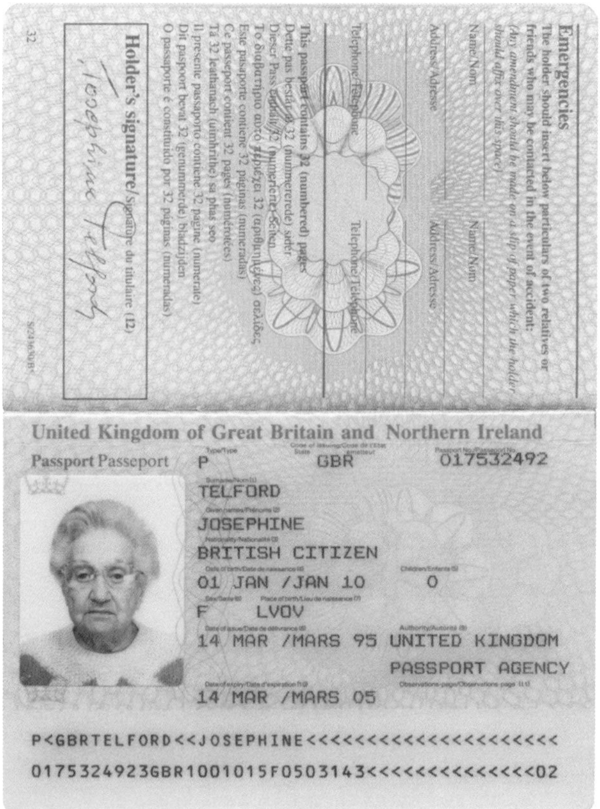

Jo's British passport.

very proud of being Austrian. As already indicated she kept aspects of her history to herself.

Answers to questions about nationality and heritage illustrate the confusion Jo felt. On some documents she states that her parents were Polish. On others she says that her father was Polish and her mother was Austrian. On one document her nationality is said to be unspecific. All of these answers were, at some point, correct.

Nothing negative was ever said to me about the time when she lived in Scotland. She told me about meeting a former fellow officer from her army days. He knew that the army was recruiting. Jo did not have to think about this for long. She re-enlisted on 26th April 1948 and joined The Scottish

End (M) Signal Regiment on 10th May 1948. The impression given was that she felt independent and 'alive' when she was in the army. Her qualification and record card gives her 'main civilian occupation' as a domestic. She made no criticism of life with her cousin but being a lodger in her cousin's house must have had its difficulties.

Something very interesting happened during that period of civilian life. On her army service and casualty form, for the second period of service, she gave her religion as Presbyterian, not Jewish. I have no details about her changing her religion. I met her when she first attended a congregational Christian chapel. She had no difficulty in fitting in with chapel services. Attendance at a Presbyterian Church would explain this.

After a few meetings with Jo we invited her to have lunch with us. She told us that her favourite food was roast pork. I remember thinking, at the time, that this was said as though it was of great significance. We were going to a restaurant and she would be able to choose her food. We later discovered that her favourite sandwiches were prawn mayonnaise. These preferences, it would appear, were to make sure that we did not suspect details of her heritage.

Chapter 8

In The Army again

Things are often said about people who have spent long periods in the armed forces not being able to adjust to civilian life. It would not be fair to say this about Jo. She was a woman who knew how to adapt and fit in. She was also thirty eight years old and unmarried. The war brought many changes for women but it was still a man's world.

Army life had been good to her. In her tin box she placed photographs of herself with fellow soldiers. They are proud and happy pictures. On the back of some of them there are the signatures of her female comrades. There are also photographs of male soldiers in wonderful dress uniforms. These are also signed. I have no information as to whether or not any of these men were 'special' to her.

Jo's stories of this period were full of fun. We would sometimes drive through Halifax and she would be reminded of something that happened.

Conscription was still in force for Jo's second period of army service. Young men, of a specific age, were called for compulsory military service. During her first period of time in the army she did some work in the pay office. The records of her second period in the army are difficult to interpret. Before looking at the records I understood that she did some similar work during this time.

This second period of army service came to an end on the 8th May 1950. Jo returned to West Yorkshire. This was an area she knew and she may have been stationed in Halifax at the time of discharge.

Chapter 9

An independent life

Jo moved to Keighley in West Yorkshire. This town is just a few miles from Bingley where she had worked as an au pair. She rented a room and found work in a mill. I do not know the name of the mill or what it produced. I assume that it produced woollen goods because, as mentioned previously, she used to take a suit length to her lawyer in Vienna. Mills employed large numbers of women and it was relatively easy to obtain employment. The work was hard and people were paid by how much they produced rather than how many hours they worked. Noise levels were very high and affected many people's hearing. Jo said that she found this work to be very hard and she soon became ill. She said that her skin was affected; particularly her fingers and nails. Jo looked after her hands. When I visited her on her one hundredth birthday I noticed that her fingernails had been polished in a very fashionable pattern.

Jo was not a person who indulged in self-pity. Having said this, she was able to convey that this period was a very low point in her life. She applied for a job near to the centre of Bradford. This was a clerical post where she would be able to use her language skills. She was successful and in January 1951 she found accommodation in the Manningham area of Bradford, near to her new workplace. This was a rented room. Of perhaps more importance was the fact that her employers understood and, at least in part, shared her history. She was able to talk to them and they cared about her. The son of that employer was present at her one hundredth birthday gathering, he had kept in regular contact with her throughout the rest of her life.

There was at least one other business in the same building as Jo's employer. Jean, who was to become a long-term friend and helper, worked there.

Jo's heart was in the countryside. She was used to hills and snow. She worked in Bradford every day from Monday to Friday and a half-day on Saturday. Every Saturday she took her rucksack and walking clothes to work. From there she used public transport to travel to Ingleton in North Yorkshire. This is an area of natural beauty with hills and streams. She met a woman who owned a café near to some caves. The caves were a tourist attraction. Jo helped the woman in the café every weekend. When Jo was in her nineties we took her back to Ingleton. She said it made her feel sad to think that she could no longer climb or walk on the rough ground near to the water. These 'leisure breaks' appeared, to me, to have been hard work. The travelling alone would have been tiring and she had to be back at work on Mondays. Nevertheless, this set a pattern for her life and all of her stories were happy ones. Jo moved home twice more in the Manningham area. My understanding is that these were rented rooms or parts of houses.

On occasion Jo would mention romance. She said that she had never met anyone who was a suitable marriage partner. I have many photographs of her as a young woman, handsome and attractive would be fair descriptions of her. There are two photographs that suggest a romantic outing. They are taken in the countryside. Both feature the same car and are clearly taken on the same occasion. On one, Jo is in the driving seat, on the other a man is standing by the car. There is no suggestion of other people being nearby. These were taken in the days when very few people owned motorcars. Jo is smartly dressed and looks very happy. I am sure that the car was not hers and she did not have a driver's license. The only record of her driving was in her army days.

In November 1961 Jo moved to the village of East Morton near Keighley, West Yorkshire. I know the road very well. From how Jo described her accommodation I think this was a small rented cottage made of Yorkshire stone. It presented some problems and on one occasion the place was flooded with water. Jo said she loved East Morton from the first moment she saw it, set in the hills above Bingley. She said it reminded her of Austria. She was still working in Bradford and used to travel to work by bus. She said that she always wore high-heeled shoes to work.

East Morton had its own social life and Jo joined in. There were a number of shops including a Co-op and a Post Office, a village hall, four Christian places of worship, a hairdressers and a pub. Employment was provided in local mills. The mills have gone, as have all of the shops. The pub is still there and now has a very smart restaurant. Jo would have loved the restaurant.

I may be giving the impression that Jo was always positive in her attitude and not one to give offence. She was friendly and throughout her

An attractive pose.

life managed to keep her friends. On the whole she was careful not to criticize authority. She was not so careful in making personal remarks. She would tell me if I had said something she did not agree with. She would sometimes make negative comments about my appearance. I noticed that she might give something away and then criticize the person for accepting it. This made me careful not to accept any of her belongings. She also made many negative comments about her landlords and the properties she rented. Despite this she managed to remain on good terms with her landlords after she had left them.

Jo became a village person. She had many friends and joined in with village activities. I did not meet her until she was an old lady but she used to tell me about New Year's Eve parties. These were all the more special because she was born on New Year's Day. Some of the parties were 'fancy dress'. She supported the organizations that helped elderly people such as delivering 'meals on wheels' and providing Christmas parties. In later life she was a guest rather than a helper at the Christmas parties, she was not over joyful at being at this end of the event.

Jo stayed with her employers in Bradford until, and after, she reached the state retirement age for women. At that time the retirement age for women was sixty years, she qualified for the state pension but she did not give up working and found a job with a firm of antique dealers in Bingley. They did some work that involved corresponding with German speaking firms. Her clerical and language skills met their needs. She was very happy working for this firm and frequently spoke about them. The firm was nearer to where she lived. She also enjoyed looking at the antiques. She owned one or two things that had some history but I never saw any evidence of antiques amongst her belongings. She worked for this firm until well into her seventies.

Jo moved to another little cottage in East Morton where she remained until moving to sheltered accommodation prior to her ninetieth birthday. She was living in this cottage when I first met her in 1987. She did a lot of moaning about this property. She said it was cold and damp and it was. There was nowhere to put a washing machine but it was near to her friends.

Shortly after I met her, the youth of the village had the habit of congregating in the bus shelter opposite to Jo's cottage. This was of great

On 19th November 1921 the emperor and his family were exiled to the Portuguese island of Madeira. He died of respiratory failure on 1st April 1922. His remains, with the exception of his heart, were interred in the Church of Our Lady of Monte. His heart, and the heart of his wife, was interred in the Monastery of Muri in Switzerland.

Jo had a photograph of herself getting into one of the famous baskets outside of the church at Monte. Travelling downhill by basket is still a Monte tourist attraction.

I never heard Jo's view on the appointment of a Polish Pope: John Paul II. On 3rd October 2004 he beatified the last Emperor of the Austro-Hungarian Empire. The last emperor, therefore, had his supporters, some of whom prayed to him and felt they were answered.

Walking, climbing and skiing were life long interests for Jo even when she could no longer partake in the activities herself. Seefeld in the Austrian Tyrol was, probably, her favourite place in the whole world. I have photographs of her, on skis, presumably in this region. There is a Seefeld address and telephone number in her address book. Her last visit to this area was made in the last few years of her life. Her friend Jean accompanied her.

Seefeld is not far from the German concentration camp at Dachau. Once again I am struck by the enormity of crimes committed against Jews. She never told me, in words, that she was Jewish so I could not ask her about her feelings when she returned to Seefeld. She gave lots of clues. The snow on the hills in her Yorkshire village reminded her of Austria. There was sadness in her voice when she said these things but I interpreted her mood as remembering happy times rather than dwelling on atrocities.

Jo travelled to European countries and to North Africa. She could remember where she had been and in which year. She was interested in other countries and their sports. She kept an eye on the Middle East and frequently talked about foreign leaders. She never criticized any of them.

Jo made use of coach tours to travel around the British Isles. She was able to do this on her own. She enjoyed the Scottish countryside and islands. One of her last journeys was to the Isle of Skye. She enjoyed the Channel Islands. She returned from these trips with information she had gleaned along the way. She collected badges and attached them to her walking stick. These reminded her of happy times.

The loss of enough strength to ski down hill was a source of sadness to Jo. She frequently criticized herself for being 'too old to do anything'.

Chapter 12

Time to leave the village

Applications for better housing had their amusing moments. We sat and worked out what should be in the letter. I typed several copies and she sent them off. Jo had been a serving member of the armed forces. The British Legion owned accommodation for elderly people. These were small apartments complete with a warden. Jo felt that her army service entitled her to one of these apartments. I tried to explain that, in all probability, someone would have to die before an apartment became available. We completed the application form and sent it off. Her application was refused on the basis that there were no apartments available. This was not a good enough explanation for Jo, she said she was going to throw her medals into the local canal.

I have seen a photograph of Jo wearing her medals at a Remembrance Day Parade. She was asked to carry a wreath of poppies and hang them on the wall of the Memorial Hall. She saw this as a great honour. She wore a fur hat and buttoned up coat. She looked serious and, in a sense, invincible. The caption 'don't mess with me' would not have been out of place. Those medals never went into the canal, I have them hanging on my wall together with a photograph of her, in uniform, with a group of female soldiers.

It took a long time before alternative accommodation was found. Eventually, she accepted a ground floor apartment provided by the local council. She made it comfortable and was soon able to acquire friends in the area. Despite being in her eighties she was able to walk into the local town of Keighley on a daily basis. She found places where she could buy a good lunch. It is no exaggeration to say that she never used her oven.

It is worth pointing out that Jo never claimed welfare benefits. She received a state pension based on her contributions. She received a pension from Austria based upon her working record in that country and the fact that she was 'persecuted by Hitler'. Jo was very grateful for pensions. She lived modestly yet comfortably and she was able to take an annual holiday.

In the application forms I completed I stressed that Jo did not have enough space to place a washing machine. She used to put her laundry into a suitcase and take it to a launderette outside the village. This entailed using the local bus. I felt strongly that this old lady should not have to struggle in order to do her washing.

The new apartment had a spacious kitchen. There was loads of room for a washing machine and I discussed with her the process of obtaining the new machine. She then started talking about spin dryers. Just in case any reader does not know about these machines, they will spin the water out of clothes but not wash them. I explained that a new washing machine would do the whole job. Jo refused this labour saving device because she enjoyed going to the launderette and talking to the lady who worked there. The new apartment was even further away from the launderette. The space made available in the kitchen was used for the permanent positioning of a clothes 'airer'. By this I mean a washing line on a metal frame. She boiled her handkerchiefs in a saucepan and eventually bought a spin dryer which she hardly ever used. She soon got used to central heating.

This new accommodation did not mean that Jo had left her village. Somebody collected her every Sunday and took her to and from chapel. If invited to a gathering she would mutter something about not being able to attend but was always there in the end.

Jo had a strong sense of independence. This did not mean that she would not ask for help. She would frequently ask someone at chapel to assist her in some way. Having said this she had made huge decisions in her life and intended to continue doing so. Around the time of her ninetieth birthday she started to talk about care homes. This was done in quite a definite way. She said she would be going into a home within the next couple of years. The way she conveyed this information did not demand pity or any kind of service. She was not expecting anyone to give her a home. In reality there was no such person available.

Jo celebrating at her ninetieth birthday party.

As time went by Jo needed and accepted more support. This included being taken to buy her shopping. She suddenly became somebody who could not sort out her own life without help. When people talked about her the word 'confused' frequently came into the conversation. I am sure that many people have been through a period in the lives of a loved one where they are not sure if the person is confused or just making their lives more interesting.

Jo's apartment was equipped with red pull cords that, if pulled, would alert a central operator. The operator, if necessary, would send someone out to help. If the cords were pulled too often, or there was no official available, they would call someone who held a key to the apartment. Well, we held the key. Late at night we might find Jo on the floor, fully dressed, next to the red cord. She was so light that I could lift her. I would perform various tasks and help her to bed. On one occasion I found that she was sleeping on her money, I am not suggesting that she had a lot of money. Of more concern was the huge carving knife under her pillow, I took the knife away and put it in the kitchen drawer. I have thought a lot about that night. This was the girl who lay behind barbed wire and threw grenades. When I discovered her knife she did not try to explain herself, she just kept her mouth shut. Had she been feeling some kind of threat that resonated with her past? I don't know. On the same night I threw away some out of date prawn sandwiches. One of those could have made her confused.

Other things happened to add weight to the theory that Jo was reliving her past. We drove through the town on Remembrance Day, we had to wait whilst the boy scouts paraded, Jo asked, "Is that the Hitler Youth?" She liked to watch tennis on television. She described someone who has been termed Britain's most loved German as 'a little Nazi'.

Amongst all of this confusion and suspicion Jo started to doubt people who were helping her. One lady had helped her with housework and shopping for some years. She helped Jo when she lived in the village and later travelled to Jo's new home, she was helpful in more ways than her job demanded. She would bring items of clothing and interesting food, these tasks far outweighed the amount of money she was paid. Jo decided that this lady was stealing her belongings. The items, allegedly, stolen were things that people would not want. On many occasions she offered me a bag of pebbles. These were pebbles she had collected on her holidays. I did not want them and refused them. I have no idea what happened to them but the lady who helped her was blamed. I suspect that she offered them to somebody who did not feel able to refuse them. Eventually, and very sadly, the lady felt she could not continue working for someone who thought she was stealing. Jo then had to rely on care organized by the local council, I make no criticism of the help given but it was nowhere near the standard she had been used to.

I found it upsetting to see a lady who had been used to having a modest lunch at a local café eating her food from a disposable tray. Lots of people did, and still do, this every day. It does not make it right.

Jo's friend Jean started to gather details about local care homes. This task was far from easy. The homes had what looked like holiday brochures. It was difficult to gather information from people who had loved ones resident within the homes. Jean found that the Austrian government was prepared to contribute to the cost of Jo's care. A huge help in all this was Jo's lawyer. He understood the needs of people in Jo's situation and was able to organize her financial affairs and cope with the many telephone calls she made to his office. She would say that she needed more money, for day-to-day living, when in fact she had more than enough.

During this period Jo telephoned me regularly. I think I was able to determine the difference between an emergency and the need for a quick chat. Jo started to talk about people stealing from her home. On one occasion a police officer called me, he said he was very experienced in dealing with people like Jo and felt sure he was correct in believing that someone had been in and had stolen her money. This might have happened. Elderly people were often encouraged to leave their doors unlocked during the day so that carers could get in. The policeman felt that I should visit her straight away. His evidence for believing her was that she did not have a purse in her bag. At that time Jo had given up on purses, following an attempt to steal from her, she had someone make special pockets in the lining of her coats so that she did not have to carry a purse. We will never know if someone had been in and stolen from her. Having young police officers investigating the situation made her life more interesting.

Jean was eventually able to organize some temporary care for Jo in a local nursing home. That stay became permanent. A group of us went to visit her on her one hundredth birthday. She had received a card from the Queen and a communication on behalf of the government. As always, she was smartly dressed, her nails had been manicured and painted in a very modern style. She did answer me when I spoke to her and thanked me for coming. She did not open her eyes throughout the whole visit. She requested that she be taken to the lavatory and a carer responded immediately. It was a sad visit but nevertheless I felt sure that Jo appreciated our efforts. I wonder if she ever used any of the gifts.

Chapter 13

Goodbye

Jo had organized her life right up to the end. She made a detailed will. This included her wish that her funeral service be held at the congregational chapel in the village where she had lived. My husband was to conduct her funeral but he predeceased her. Fortunately, she was quite lucid when I spoke to her about this. It was agreed that I would take his place. The funeral service was to be followed by a committal at the crematorium. When Jo spoke about this she said, “They can just take me and ash me”. I wondered if these words, in some way, resonated with what, in all probability, had happened to her mother.

Jo left all of her money to two charities. We used to watch a quiz program on the television. She used to say that if she were able to take part and win she would give the money to the same two charities.

We did not know if many people would attend Jo’s funeral. We made arrangements with a local restaurant for meals to be provided to order. A large number of people attended the service and a smaller number accepted the meal. I felt this was a fitting ending. Jo rewarded people who were kind to her by buying them a meal. On the day of her funeral she did it ‘one last time’.

Well, all those changing borders. What nationality was Josephine Tramer who became Josephine Telford? The answer is easy. Without fear of contradiction, she was British. She was proud of this country and, for that matter, so am I.

Well done, Josephine Tramer!

TRAMER FAMILY TREE

Solomon Kraus
m. **Fanni Schwarz.**

Klara Kraus
b. 9/9/1883.
Did not survive
the Riga camp.

Mark Tramer
m. **Perl.**

Moses Tramer
b. 18/8/1873
Evidence of grave in the
Bielsko Jewish Cemetery
Poland. Died 1939 aged 66.

Married in a Jewish Ceremony in Vienna, Austria on 26th June 1907. Moved to Silesia, Southern Poland when it was still part of the Austro-Hungarian Empire.

Josephine Tramer born in Lvov Poland, now Ukraine, 1/1/1910. Came to England from Vienna in 1939. Served in the British Army in war and peace time. She was awarded the France and Germany Star. She became a Corporal. She died in a care home in Yorkshire, England in 2010 having reached her centenary.

ABOUT THE AUTHOR

Annie Louisa Harrison, originally from North Staffordshire, was born in 1952. It was a great time to be born. The war was over and rationing had almost come to an end. In her lifetime huge progress was to be made in comfort and technology. More people, than ever before, were allowed to travel the world. Never mind the world, the motorcar opened up all kinds of freedom. Progress was made in allowing women to realize their potential in the workplace. Higher education was free.

Born to working class parents, there was never an alternative to earning one's living. Her father was a coal miner and her mother worked in a mill making soldiers' uniforms. They were able to move area and find different types of employment. Her mother became a trades' union official.

As a young child, maternal grandparents played a significant role. Her grandmother had been a servant and told stories about working in other people's houses. These were peppered with comments about status and people thinking they were better than everyone else. Annie loved the stories and did not mind them being repeated. A thirst for real stories, about real people, began.

Her grandfather found that he had a little shadow. He took her on walks and all outings came with some kind of treat. He had become a Christian in adult life and he had no time for arguments between denominations. He, therefore, had no problem with her preference for simple church services without ritual. Together they might go to a Methodist service, choral evensong and to hear the Salvation Army band. He taught her to treat everyone the same, regardless of race or creed. He 'gave her away' on her wedding day.

The system of education in the central midlands had the facility of allowing pupils, dependent upon passing the eleven plus examination, to attend schools anywhere in the city. She attended a girls' school. One uniform fitted for the whole five years. Some pupils boasted high status parents. One of her friends, not high status, became a secretary of state. The school leaving age, at that time, was fifteen. Staying at school for an extra year made a significant difference when applying for a job. Interests outside of school, added to the fact that she obtained a position some months before leaving, meant that little work was done for the exams. She obtained two 'O' levels, English and Art. Of course, no revision was necessary. No employer ever asked to see the certificates. The first job was in banking. It would be fair to say that she hated this job and the next two. Rules, unfair treatment of customers, poor pay and sheer boredom were not to her taste.

Annie married a week before her twentieth birthday owing to the fact that holidays in Menorca were cheaper that week! The couple had nearly thirty four years of happy marriage before her husband died of cancer. The years were not wasted. They got rid of the debts that hold back young people and both studied for degrees. She went to the lectures and studied hard. Being a student was so good she thought of failing her exams so that she could stay another year. A degree in applied social science opened doors for the author to work with people who find themselves in difficulty. There was never any looking back. She was able to listen to people from all walks of life tell their stories.

The elements of her life can be seen in the author's fictional work. *Somebody's Love* (published on Kindle) tells the story of a man who wants to have status, in doing this he convinces few people and hurts the people who love him. *Nobody's Child* (also Kindle) explores the issue of romantic love being no match for family and society rules. Both books explore the role of the state in dictating our lives.

Moving Borders is a different kind of work. Still motivated by a good story, this one is out of respect to the subject who, in not so many words, gave instruction for her story to be written. She left documents and clues. This book is for her.

If retirement means doing nothing, the author has yet to retire. Retirement and widowhood are gifts. No need to negotiate, just go and do it. She has had a lifelong love of tennis and started to play in her mid fifties. She started to play the piano in her thirties. Guitar playing is a few months old. No degree of competence is claimed in any of these pursuits. If you have a love of history you will regularly find her guiding visitors through a Warwickshire National Trust property.

Where does the writing come from? It is nothing to do with the writing. It is a head full of stories.